SEIZE
the
FIRE

ALSO BY RICHARD FLANAGAN

FICTION

Death of a River Guide

The Sound of One Hand Clapping

Gould's Book of Fish

The Unknown Terrorist

Wanting

The Narrow Road to the Deep North

First Person

NON-FICTION

Notes on an Exodus

SEIZE

the

FIRE

THREE
SPEECHES

RICHARD
FLANAGAN

PENGUIN BOOKS

PENGUIN BOOKS

UK | USA | Canada | Ireland | Australia
India | New Zealand | South Africa | China

Penguin Books is part of the Penguin Random House group of companies
whose addresses can be found at global.penguinrandomhouse.com.

First published by Penguin Random House Australia Pty Ltd 2018

Cover design by Alex Ross © Penguin Random House Australia Pty Ltd
Author photograph by Joel Saget
Typeset in Bembo by Midland Typesetters, Australia
Printed and bound in Australia by Griffin Press, an accredited
ISO AS/NZS 14001 Environmental Management Systems printer.

 A catalogue record for this
book is available from the
National Library of Australia

ISBN 978 0 14379 532 2

penguin.com.au

CONTENTS

Contents

Author's Note

Gathered here are three speeches I have made in recent years. Of a moment, they live or die with the crowd, for audiences are nervous creatures, easily startled, quick to unsettle, liable to stampede.

From the first word the audience must feel confident that they can relax, listen, think and dream. The audience must believe that the speaker will not embarrass them should they decide to laugh or cry or grow passionate; nor yet let them down, or confuse them by seeming to say one thing only for it to become apparent they mean the opposite, or possibly nothing much at all.

And to achieve this, to hold the crowd, in order not to bore, my speeches tend to be written the day and night and moments before being given, larded with the topical, from local sport to the day's controversies and scandals.

For that reason I have chosen in this book not to rid these speeches of the marks of their making, the small change of topical jokes and allusions, as the words of each speech are finally a unity conceived and written as a whole and impossible to untangle without destroying something fundamental.

And it is that fundamental thing that I hope justifies the publication of these three speeches. But what is it?

This book's title is taken from William Blake's poem 'The Tyger'. It is his most famous and perhaps his most elusive poem. Who is the God, Blake appears to be asking, who could create, as well as the gentle lamb, the fearful tiger; the God who could seize the fire and transform it into the tiger's burning eyes?

The poem seems to paradoxically answer that God is our ability to transmute horror by describing it, to transcend evil by framing the tiger's 'fearful symmetry'. Among the many attributes of such a God is the man who out of this fire creates such a poem.

More than ever we need to name our own dread tigers so that we can know them, in order that we might survive them, so that we might create something better from them.

There is, of course, an alternative.

But if these speeches have an argument it is this: allowing the fire to seize and devour us is no alternative at all.

It is *we* who must seize the fire.

On Love Stories
and Reza Barati

CLOSING ADDRESS, PERTH WRITERS FESTIVAL, 23 FEBRUARY 2014

Hobart, I discovered flying here the other day, is a thousand kilometres more distant from Perth than Moscow is from London. Misunderstanding the significance of these sorts of distances accounts for a great deal of horror and defeat in human history. Such expanses of space between ambition and achievement have put a summary end to the ambitions of many of the great. Napoleon. Hitler. The Sydney Swans.

Admittedly, I haven't come here with delusions of conquest, but only to deliver this closing address about love stories. But I am feeling the same sense of unease as Napoleon must have felt when, finally camped in Moscow, he saw the first flames leap up around the Kremlin's fairytale onion domes. As Kieren Jack presumably felt at the beginning of the third quarter when something came between him and the sun. And it was Ryan Crowley.

There are several reasons for my unease.

Rainer Maria Rilke was admittedly not a Dockers tagger, but a sort of European equivalent, a German poet—in many respects a charlatan masquerading as a genius who turned out to be a genius. He cultivated anyone he could sponge off—women, the titled, the rich or, ideally, rich titled women. Once, according to an account from Kenneth Rexroth, Rilke was 'leaning gracefully against the mantelpiece in a castle in Switzerland while his devoted duchesses and countesses and other disciples were passionately discussing Goethe's *Faust*, a discussion in which Rilke was taking no part whatsoever. One of them turned to him and asked, "How do you feel about *Faust*, master?" To which Rilke answered, "I have never been able to read more than a page of it."'

In truth, not unlike Rilke, there are many great books and great love stories that I have never been able to get past the first page of. And then there are even more I have never even started. And the more I read, the greater, I guess, grows the library of unread books. Of all the love stories ever published, I have—realistically—read very few. My despair, then, in realising I had agreed to talk about love stories for some extended period was great. For I am no expert on love stories.

Then there is the matter of love itself; love, a word so trammelled by overuse as to be almost senseless. We like love, we *love* love, but perhaps its only meaning lies in its ubiquitous meaninglessness. We apprehend it, we feel it, and we think we know it, yet we cannot say what we mean by it. Like Elvis, it's frequently sighted in unusual locations—the Balga KFC, say, carrying several bags of half-eaten chicken nuggets, or the Mirrabooka Hungry Jack's leaning out of a beaten-up HiLux dual cab—but vanishes at the point at which we seek to authenticate it as real. We bury love under the rubble of other words and sentiments, deluding ourselves that such gravel is gravitas, to make it seem as if we do know what love means.

To give you but one example: St Paul's First Letter to the Corinthians, Chapter 13. Its justly famed and poetic evocation of love is perhaps the most popular biblical reading at contemporary wedding ceremonies.

Yet in the Greek original, the word that is commonly translated into English as the word 'love' is the word *agape* (are-gar-pee). What *agape* meant in the ancient world is open to debate—it was about love of spouse or family, and contrasted with the word and idea of *philia*, which suggested friendship, fraternity and so on—and *eros*—which was sexual attraction. The authors of the

King James Bible, following the example of Wycliffe's seminal English translation, chose the word 'charity' as the correct translation of *agape*. What did St Paul really want us to think on our wedding days? That the best we could hope for was that our spouses might view us charitably?

Or, was what he was writing simply beautiful wordplay? Did it mean anything at all? What would happen if we substituted some other word for *agape* instead of love?

What would happen if it had been, say, a football coach writing to one of his team's sports scientists, under the excited misapprehension that *agape* was, in fact, classical Greek for training supplements used by the ancient Olympians, and offering the following new version of St Paul's letter?

Though I speak with the tongues of men and of angels and have not peptides, I am become as a sounding brass, or a tinkling cymbal. And though I have the gift of prophecy, and understand all mysteries, and all knowledge; and though I have all faith, so that I could remove mountains, and have not peptides, I am nothing. And though I bestow all my goods to feed the poor, and though I give my body to be burned, and have not peptides, it profiteth me nothing. Peptides suffereth long, and is kind;

peptides envieth not; peptides vaunteth not itself, is not puffed up, doth not behave unseemly, seeketh not her own, is not easily provoked, thinketh no evil; rejoiceth not in iniquity, but rejoiceth in the truth; beareth all things, believeth all things, hopeth all things, endureth all things ... And now abideth faith, hope, peptides, these three; but the greatest of these is peptides.

A small aside here about a contemporary mistranslation of love: I was moved to read that the previous British prime minister, David Cameron, used to sign off all his text messages to Rebekah Brooks with 'LOL', presuming it meant 'lots of love'.

Back, though, in that near mystical time when people still communicated in words rather than acronyms of idiocy, Vincent Van Gogh wrote to his brother Theo, 'What a mystery life is, and love the mystery within the mystery.'

And here is the second reason for my unease talking here today: I can offer nothing to say about that mystery within the mystery. Of love I know only the same as anyone else in this room—the same confusions and disappointments and ecstasies, the same memories of abandonment and return, the same sense of grace lost and of grace found. My subject tonight is far more limited: love stories.

My interest in them grew pointed when I began to write the novel that was to become *The Narrow Road to the Deep North*. I have talked far too much in too many interviews about the personal origins of that novel in the war experiences of my father. But, like all novels, its beginnings were at once complex and simple.

I had known for a long time that one day I would have to write a book that encompassed not the war then, but the war my father carried with him, the war that we, his family, ended up carrying within us. And I knew I needed some leaven, some light, to ensure the story not collapse under the weight of its darkness. For in the end all human life aspires to hope, the highest expression of which is love. Without hope, there is no future. And slowly, very slowly, I came to understand that for my novel to be true to this hope that is the nub of us as human beings, to make this story of war work, I needed to write a love story.

This was a terrifying revelation.

I had long wanted to write a love story, and I had long—wisely, I felt—shirked the challenge, because I felt it the hardest story of all to write. No one can say what love is in any precise way, yet we know it—know it so powerfully that we recognise any false notes in its descriptions. And one bad note and we dismiss the novel. Readers, I had learned, will forgive you many failings as a writer. But not when it comes to love. This failure—to be untrue to that enigma at our centre—the reader will reward only by throwing the book across the room.

And so I began collecting love stories from those I met, late at night, in bars in distant cities, in phone calls, and casual conversations over coffee. I paid more attention when reading love stories. I was trying to understand what a love story was. And all this led me to several discoveries.

The first was that a love story in life is not the same as a love story in a book.

In these strangely solipsistic times, it is falsely presumed a writer's own feeling is everything in art. It is not. Art has to have form, or it is nothing. A novel without form is a jellyfish pretending to be a white pointer. Love though, is anything but form—it is a chaotic, bewildering sense of abandonment; real, dirty, mad; a lost mind, a rapturously empty stomach; a gasp of unknowing knowing-all; a confusion of events.

Love stories, on the other hand, are galley slaves that must row to the unforgiving beat of structure and action. They must have the force of parable and the incantatory spell of fable. A love story, more than most stories, needs the most careful shaping, a strange combination of high inspiration and low cunning. If love is a cracked compass with no north, a love story must be a lodestone that leads inevitably to its own conclusion.

Visiting Sydney in 2001 for the publication of *Gould's Book of Fish*, I was one day walking across the Sydney Harbour Bridge when a story came to my mind that my parents often told. It was about a Latvian man who lived in the small country town of Longford where I was born. Swept up in the convulsions that created the bloodlands of Eastern Europe during the war, he managed to make his way back at the war's end to his Latvian village only to find it razed to the ground and his young wife, he was told, dead. He refused to believe this was so. For the next two years he searched the wastelands of postwar Europe—the East, the West, the DP centres, the Red Cross camps—for his wife, all to no avail. He finally had to accept the terrible truth: she had perished. He immigrated to Australia, came to live in Longford, married and had a family.

In 1957 he visited Sydney. Strolling down a crowded street he saw walking towards him his Latvian wife, alive, with a child on either hand. At that moment he had to decide whether he would acknowledge her or walk on by.

This very beautiful story had always moved me. And I thought how—if I could transform that story by having a returned POW seeing a lover he thought dead walking across that very bridge I now was walking across—I would then have the key I needed to write the novel.

But immediately the question arose: how to make of this image a love story? So began a quixotic—I choose the term carefully—twelve-year exploration of what a love story truly is.

My study of love stories, haphazard as it was, led me early to the troubadours of medieval Provence. Their stories are frequently absurd and ridiculous. 'What do the troubadours have to say to us today?' Roberto Bolaño once asked, to answer, 'They invented love, and they also invented or reinvented the pride of being a writer, of gazing fearlessly into the depths.'

In an obscure memorial volume I found a reprint of a lecture given by Vyvyan Holland in 1953 to an enigmatic dining society known as the Sette of Odd Volumes on the subject of courts of love, a phenomenon that flourished in twelfth- and thirteenth-century Provence.

Holland describes how at first the courts of love were an extension of the entertainment of troubadours, and troubadours would dispute with each other in song and verse, over questions of love and what was and what wasn't appropriate behaviour. These contests were held before assemblies of ladies that called themselves 'courts of love'.

Questions were argued back and forth, and in their judgements the courts of love took as their authority the Code of Love, thirty-one rules of amorous entanglement, the origins of which are lost in obscurity. Some of the rules are:

Marriage is not a bar to loving someone else.

A true lover is not indiscreet.

Love constantly either increases or diminishes.

At first the disputes were little more than academic entertainments constructed around hypothetical cases, but as time went on, according to Holland, a case law of love arose, which people would use to win arguments or to explain, praise or condemn behaviour. Slowly the courts of love began dealing also with real cases of love. Holland finds several things striking about the courts of love—their beauty and pageantry; that they were an expression of women's power; and the way in which they formally recognised love as more important than marriage, an institution acknowledged at the time to be only tangentially connected with love.

I had a longstanding interest in Holland that went back many years to when I was sixteen, working as a surveyor's chainman. I would drop into Mr Browser's Secondhand Bookshop in Liverpool Street, Hobart, a few minutes before I caught my bus home. Between the shop window and a dingy curtain which bisected the bookshop some two-thirds of the way back were to be found the books. But Mr Browser's Secondhand

Bookshop also replicated the old Greek separation between *agape* and *eros* by the device of the curtain, above which the more keen-eyed would spot a small, finely fly-specked sign that read 'Gentleman's Literature'— and behind which were to be found furtive customers with the sad eyes of startled marsupials looking up from the racks of second-hand pornography on which they silently grazed.

Writing this I am struck with wonder at having once lived in a time and place so poor that it was possible to make a living out of selling used pornography. When in these times of marvel we talk about the transformation of the retail industry I always feel a little rheumy-eyed thinking of such halcyon days as those that would support such enterprise.

But let us drop the curtain on *eros* and return to the *agape* section of our talk. It was in the front of Mr Browser's Secondhand Bookshop that I came upon Vyvyan Holland's memoirs. Holland, I read, was the younger of Oscar Wilde's two sons, born in 1886. His book was a revelation to me, who only knew the broad outlines of Wilde's fame, stories and terrible fall.

Holland describes a loving father who both he and his brother Cyril adored, a man very far from the Victorian patriarchs of the era who, writes Holland, 'delighted in playing our games' in the nursery and all over the house, at the beach building sand castles, 'an art', writes

Holland, 'at which he excelled; long rambling castles they were, with moats and tunnels and towers and battlements, and when they were finished, he would usually pull a few lead soldiers out of his pocket to man the walls'.

Holland remembered his father telling he and Cyril of 'the family house at Moytura, where he was going to take us one day, and of "the great melancholy carp" in Lough Corrib, that never moved from the bottom of the lough unless he called them with Irish songs learnt from his father; and he would sing these songs to us. I don't think he sang very well, but to us he had the most beautiful voice in the world . . . he invented poems in prose for us which, though we may not have always understood their inner meaning, always held us spellbound'.

After Wilde's imprisonment and disgrace in consequence of his love affair with Lord Alfred Douglas, known to Wilde and history more generally as the feckless Bosie, his children were taken from him, and their names changed to that of their mother's family. During his father's trial in the spring of 1895, Vyvyan and Cyril Holland were withdrawn from their schools, much as Wilde's books were being withdrawn from the bookshops and libraries. Cyril was sent to stay with family in Ireland where he read newspapers left lying around.

'He was terribly distressed,' wrote Holland many years later, 'and the hackneyed expression "he never smiled again" was for him almost true . . . Shortly before he was killed by a German sniper in the first war he wrote to me: "I was nine years old when I saw the first placard. You were there too, but you did not see it. It was in Baker Street. I asked what it meant and I received an evasive answer. I never rested until I found out."'

The children were sent to France. 'My mother remained behind to be of what assistance she could to my father,' Holland writes, 'until she too was driven from her home by the entrance of the bailiff's men, and the subsequent sale of all the contents of the house. That sale was a scandalous piece of barefaced robbery. Even before it took place, the house was full of riff-raff, souvenir hunting and stealing anything they could lay their hands upon . . . Among them were first editions of all my father's books with inscriptions to my mother, to my brother and to myself, which were kept in my mother's bedroom, in a special bookcase to the right of the door . . .

'For months afterwards, my brother and I kept asking for our soldiers, our trains and other toys, and we could not understand why it upset our mother, since of course we knew nothing about the sale. It was only when I saw the catalogue, many years later, that I realised why my mother had been upset. The sale consisted of 246 lots;

number 237 was "A large quantity of toys"; they realised thirty shillings.'

Holland, also a soldier, survived the war and then survived the peace, living off his father's royalties. He wrote a little; modest, almost homely pieces, though one senses in his works a soul intimidated by the brilliance of his father. Like all the best writing, everything that matters is left out.

Ernest Hemingway once wrote a love story about he and his wife getting a train ride back to Paris. The tone is strange, dissociated. There is a mood of change, but nothing happens. In the final paragraph the train arrives in Paris, and they get off, heading to different houses, because their marriage has ended. At that point you understand exactly what the story is about.

Vyvyan Holland's paper to the Sette of Odd Volumes dining society on the subject of courts of love is somewhat similar. Holland's whole life was shaped by the tragedy imposed on his father by a court of law. Reading his thoughts on the courts of love, you cannot escape the notion that he is thinking how different would his father's life, his life, his brother's and mother's life have been if Wilde had been tried in a court of love; if his judges had been women, their reference not English common law, but the code of love.

For who, or what, exactly, is Holland writing about when he describes how:

Beauty and love were worshipped in that golden happy land that was Provence in its half-childish, half-pagan state before it was wrecked and tortured by fanatical northern barbarians in the fourteenth century . . . The invading clergy destroyed vast quantities of Provencal poetry and literature . . . in their attempt to abolish the heresies of poetry, gaiety and love.

It is as if he is trying to sing 'the great melancholy carp' home from the bottom of Lough Corrib, calling him with songs learned from his father.

And thinking on this, I thought of how no love story—whether it is Wilde's for Bosie, or anyone else's for that matter—is ever simply, or only, about their love story. For love is many things, and at a certain point it is the universe. As well as Bosie, Wilde loved his children, his children him; his wife also. His warder in Reading Gaol wrote in *Bruno's Weekly* of 22 January 1916 of the experience of guarding Wilde in gaol, describing how wretched he felt having to shave Wilde's head of his famous long hair as the writer wept:

The saddest story I know of Wilde was one day when his solicitor called to see him to get his signature, I think, to some papers in the divorce proceedings then being instituted by his wife—a suit which, of course, Wilde did not defend.

Unknown to Wilde, his wife had accompanied the solicitor, but she did not wish her husband to see her. The interview with the solicitor took place in the consultation room, and Wilde sat at a table with his head on his hands.

Outside, in the passage with me, waited a sad figure in deepest mourning. It was Mrs Wilde—in tears.

Whilst the consultation was proceeding in the solicitor's room, Mrs Wilde turned to me and begged a favour. 'Let me have one glimpse of my husband,' she said, and I could not refuse her.

So silently I stepped on one side, Mrs Wilde cast one long, lingering glance inside, and saw the convict poet, who in deep mental distress himself, was totally unconscious that any eyes save that of his stern lawyer and myself witnessed his degradation.

A second later, Mrs Wilde, apparently labouring under deep emotion, drew back and left the prison . . . I do not know if she ever saw her unhappy husband again. I do not think she ever did.

Reading this story I wondered, what is a love story? Where does it begin? Where does it end? What is its essential nature?

Here is a love story written three thousand years ago:

You burn me.

Those three words are the only surviving fragment of a poem by the Greek poet Sappho, and yet they are also a complete love story. It works, because it obeys the first and greatest rule of love stories: it is true. And it is true because it tells the reader everything and answers nothing. Who? Where? What? All irrelevant. The essential nature of a love story is that it is true.

This brings me to a second characteristic I noticed about so many love stories that moved me: they were always concerned with the limits of literature's ability to describe life in general and love in particular. The troubadours' songs of courtly love inspired the Italian *dolce stil novo*—the sweet new style that Dante both named and made his own with *The Divine Comedy*, which had the additional effect—for the first time since Rome—of elevating the vernacular to the highest levels of expression. The idea of love and love of language were already coming together to form a new idea of literature.

There was, of course, a reaction to the idea of courtly love, with its ever more absurd adoration of women as divine objects, and it takes the form of the first great modern novel, *Don Quixote*, in which the self-appointed knight of La Mancha sets out with a chamber pot on his head, deluded by his reading of books of courtly love and chivalry, choosing Aldonza Lorenzo, a brawny, lusty local farmgirl, as his lady love, naming her Dulcinea del Toboso, a noblewoman for whom he invents an aristocratic lineage. The modern novel thus begins with the idea that books are an illusion, that they take you away from life, and no more so than when they deal with love.

Don Quixote—both a creation and victim of books about love—finally comes to realise he is being written about, recovers his sanity as he is dying, and has a will made in which he has a clause advising that his niece be disinherited should she ever marry a man who reads books of chivalry.

In Don Quixote's madness is born the strange dance that goes on ever after in the novel, between the damaging unreality of literature and the tragedy of love.

The one thing that never seems to work in a love story is the language of love itself, which is, as Don Quixote discovered, a delusion and a dangerous lie. It was almost as if the more love stories pointed out the limits of language, the more they succeeded in communicating the incommunicable experience of love. This tendency becomes particularly noticeable in the nineteenth century when the novel is experiencing a revolution in form, technique and popularity. In 1856, Gustave Flaubert publishes *Madame Bovary*, which is, in one sense, a tragic take on the comic story of *Don Quixote*. Like the noble knight, Emma Bovary is a victim of romantic literature. Flaubert writes:

Before her marriage Emma had thought that she had love within her grasp, but since the happiness which she had expected this love to bring her hadn't come, she supposed she must have been mistaken. And Emma tried to imagine just what was meant, in life, by the words 'bliss', 'passion', and 'rapture'—words that had seemed so beautiful to her in books.

Later in his seminal novel, Flaubert does something very unexpected. He, the writer who believed if you just searched long enough, worked hard enough, you could always find exactly the right word or words to express yourself, steps out of character, out of the novel itself and, anticipating the new age of the novel that is no longer certain of anything, admits to the impossibility of his central belief as a writer: Why is it, Flaubert writes, 'that fullness of soul can sometimes overflow in utter vapidity of language, for none of us can ever express the exact measure of his needs or his thoughts or his sorrows; and all human speech is like a cracked kettle on which we tap crude rhythms for bears to dance to, when all the time we long to move the stars to pity.'

Love stories are inevitably crude rhythms tapped on cracked kettles—the paradox is that when they succeed they do move the stars to pity. And we with them.

This strange sense of a book being forever inadequate to a love story is given its greatest expression twenty-one years after Emma Bovary fretted about what exactly passion was, following perhaps the most celebrated death scene in the history of the novel—when Anna Karenina throws herself under a train.

This chapter is much commented and glossed about. Never mentioned though is the chapter that succeeds it, in which Levin's brother finally publishes his book *An Essay in the Survey of The Principles and Forms of Statehood in Europe and Russia*, fully expecting the book 'to make a serious impression in society and cause, if not a revolution in scholarship, at least a great stir in the scholarly world'. Nothing happens. No one notices. There are not even reviews. And in this strange way—this startling contrast between the suicide of an unknown woman fallen from grace, and the publication of a grand book about great things—Tolstoy seems to be pointing to the essential absurdity of books.

In Tolstoy's calculus, Anna's death matters infinitely more than a book which, finally, is without the fundamental power of life. And yet the paradox is this: it has taken us reading a book to know this.

By our times, this sense of the limitation of words has been taken several steps further. From the cryptic title of Ray Carver's 'What We Talk About When We Talk About Love', to its flat setting—a dinner party of two couples in Albuquerque in which, as they slowly get drunk after dinner swapping stories about love—the enigma of love is addressed obliquely and tangentially. A strange unease enters the room after Mel, a cardiologist, tells the story of an old couple who come into the hospital after a car accident. Both are badly injured and covered in plaster casts. And Mel discovers the old man is depressed not because of the pain but because the casts prevent him from looking at his wife:

> 'He said that was making him feel so bad. Can you imagine? I'm telling you, the man's heart was breaking because he couldn't turn his goddam head and see his goddam wife.'
>
> Mel looked around the table and shook his head at what he was going to say.
>
> 'I mean it was killing the old fart just because he couldn't look at the fucking woman.'

The story ends with the evening becoming strangely awkward and a growing sense that Mel is depressed. It may be he is depressed from not being able to see his kids from his first marriage. The story leaves that open as a possibility, but there is no definite conclusion. It's just possible that Mel may no longer love his wife, Terri. Or that he feels their love is somehow not enough. That he doesn't know love like the old man. Carver's story, like life, is suddenly spilling into the universe as Mel turns his glass over on the table, spilling gin:

'Gin's gone,' Mel said.

Terri said, 'Now what?'

I could hear my heart beating. I could hear everyone's heart. I could hear the human noise we sat there making, not one of us moving, not even when the room went dark.

There is an enigma in Carver's final words that points to the greater enigma of love stories: the deeper we go into a love story the less it seems to be about love; and the more love seems to be making us think about so much that is not love. Chekhov ends a tale of an adulterous affair in the love story I think is one of the greatest, 'Lady with Lapdog', in the most remarkable way:

He and Anna Sergeevna loved each other like very close, dear people, like husband and wife, like tender friends; it seemed to them that fate itself had destined them for each other, and they could not understand why he had a wife and she a husband; and it was as if they were two birds of passage, caught and forced to live in different cages . . .

And it seemed as though in a little while the solution would be found, and then a new, beautiful life would begin; and it was clear to both of them that the end was still far, far off, and that the most complicated and difficult part was just beginning.

What does Chekhov mean? That they will succeed? Or that they must fail? That love is doomed or love is triumphant? Or does he mean that love is not life, and that now they are returning to life, love is no longer a guide to anything?

Love, to borrow Hitchcock's term, is frequently the MacGuffin—the red herring—that drives the story forward. *The Great Gatsby*, for example, is a most curious melodrama, an unbelievable farce—the love story of which is completely implausible but utterly necessary in transforming a creaking plot into a great novel.

In the end, love remains ever more elusive. The more we think of love stories like *Anna Karenina* or that contemporary masterpiece, Alice Munro's 'The Bear Came Over the Mountain'—a short story of a man watching his wife lose her mind and then, in front of him in the aged care home, no longer recognising who her husband is and falling in love with another man—the more we read love stories, the more we realise that what we are reading about, when we read about love, is not love, but life itself.

Which brings me to death. In his almost perfectly structured love story 'Spring in Fialta', Vladimir Nabokov teases us with hints we do not recognise until the final line when we discover the narrator's beloved, Nina, has died in a car smash, and the whole story has been an elegy.

Not every love story worth its mettle has a death. But so many do, and without death they would make no sense at all. Romeo and Juliet saved? Hardly. Yuri Zhivago surviving seeing Lara from his Moscow tram would see *Dr Zhivago*, the novel, peter out even more miserably than Lara perishing in the Gulag. Anna Karenina, the woman, living, is *Anna Karenina*, the novel, mortally wounded.

Tolstoy, who had the most extraordinary instincts as a storyteller, once wrote a story called *The Devil* about a landowner's love affair with one of the peasant women who worked on his estate. Though he marries, he is unable to shake off the extraordinary attraction the woman holds over him. The story—with strong autobiographical elements—was one Tolstoy struggled to finish. His original ending had the landowner kill himself; a second ending, written twenty years later, had the landowner kill the woman.

Both endings work by using death to demonstrate the great truth about love: that we discover eternity in a moment that dies immediately after. Love dies; thus we need the death of one of the lovers in a love story.

Yet trapping the moment in space and time is the guarantee that not a kiss or look is lost. Through language, and only through language, can love, ephemeral in nature, become eternal in story. Time, as

W. H. Auden wrote, 'worships language and forgives/ Everyone by whom it lives'.

Language endures, love stories endure with it, and buried in them Trojan horse-like is an alternative, better idea of what it is to be human than those presently offered by our leaders. And perhaps it is this that explains why love stories—tales of the small, the private and the intimate—are so resonant with societies in periods of inequality and injustice.

In the desert of our politics, where to show compassion for our fellow humans and to speak of kindness as a touchstone of civilisation is to threaten our borders with invasion; in what sometimes feels to be the prison of these days where those whose job it is to find truth are warned by the powerful to praise power, not question it; at such a place and time we can do worse than seek to reaffirm in love stories our fundamental sense of who and what we are.

For crammed into love stories are not just assignations, betrayals, setbacks and occasional ecstasy, not only hate and pain and horror, to say nothing of death and forgetting, but also a larger idea of our humanity.

And crowded between the discovery of ourselves in others and of others in ourselves, we sometimes glimpse something else on the horizon, a promise or threat; it is hard at first to know. Today it takes the form of a battered, shuddering boat, and on the boat, jammed between the blue polytarp thrown over the shivering, the sunburnt and the silent, caught between the briny largeness of the sea and the sky, terrifying and hopeful, breathing in the nauseating oily drifts of diesel fumes, there stands a tall twenty-three-year-old Iranian called Reza Barati, who dares dream that freedom and safety will soon be his as the boat of refugees approaches the Australian territory of Christmas Island.

But the sky darkens, the idea cannot hold, the ocean shimmers and transforms into something terrible, and all that remains of that dream is a white plastic chair Barati now holds up in front of his face, seeking to ward off the inexplicable blows of machetes and bullets and boots—a white plastic chair, all that a rich nation that prides itself on a fair go, on its largeness of spirit, has left for Barati to defend his life against those who have now come to kill him.

In the silence that now passes for our public life, a silence only broken by personal vilification of anyone who posits an idea opposed to power, it is no longer wise for a public figure to express concern about a society that sees some human beings as no longer human; a society that has turned its back on those who came to us for asylum—that is, for freedom, and for safety. And so, with our tongues torn we are expected to agree with the silence, with the lies, and with the murder of Reza Barati.

Will our prime minister say of this death what he so recently said of human rights abuses in Sri Lanka, 'We accept that sometimes in difficult circumstances, difficult things happen.' It would be condemned as not showing affection for our national team were a public figure to repeat the story of the Tamil woman, Vasantha—as reported by the BBC at the time of the prime minister's comments—who describes being 'kicked, beaten with batons and pipes, burned with hot wires and cigarettes, submerged in a barrel of water until she thought she would drown, suffocated by having a petrol-soaked plastic bag put over her head, before being repeatedly raped by men in [Sri Lankan] army uniform', the torture and rape going on for twenty days 'before a relative could find her and pay a bribe for her release'.

It would be even more foolish to not accept that human beings crowded like animals without hope in a compound on a hellish island is perfectly right and civilised, as right and civilised as the language of politicians of both parties who now publicly boast that it is good and necessary to be cruel. This is the most wicked poison to ask any society to drink, and yet we are drinking it, and drinking it to the full.

Humankind survives and prospers through a paradox so terrible we generally refuse to acknowledge it: on the one hand as groups, we sanction and promote the most terrible crimes to benefit the group's interest. Every day states and corporations do things which, were we to do them as individuals, would lead us to be sent to jail. Or, at the very least, to be despised as a human being without a shred of decency or goodness.

On the other, we jog along individually through acts of kindness and goodness. By and large, occasional acts of violence aside, we do not as individuals behave with each other as we do as groups. That is our saving grace. This paradox is also, I think, the hidden dynamic of love stories.

And perhaps it is because love stories point to the fundamental divide within us—between the mystic echoes of the individual soul, which craves freedom, and the dictates of community, which demand conformity to codes and practices we frequently find objectionable and sometimes profoundly wrong. In a sense this is a war that is waged in every human heart, and each human life makes its way through the rubble-strewn no-man's-land that arises in our souls in consequence, trying to live as best we can.

For this reason love stories tend to often be transgressive and subversive or, in the parlance of back cover blurbs, star-crossed. Love that occurs in forbidden no-man's-land—adulterous love, same-sex love or love between races or castes, as is the case in Bohumil Hrabal's classic *Too Loud a Solitude*, where the Czech book-compressor Hanta falls in love with a Gypsy girl who we discover was killed by the Nazis.

Hrabal was a hero of Milan Kundera's, whose own tales of erotic love in the totalitarian ruins of Czechoslovakia speak more powerfully of the terrible human costs of a world where everything is political, while at the same time challenging that perverted understanding of life by pointing to the places of the soul the state did not penetrate or control.

In this, George Orwell's *Nineteen Eighty-Four* has been decisive in reshaping the love story for our times: Winston's love for Julia is the revolt the Thought Police fear most. To break Winston politically, they have to destroy Winston's love of Julia in Room 101 of the Ministry of Love. Politics, in our times, has become the enemy of love.

Like Kundera's Czechoslovaks, we must seek to rediscover ourselves in the language of love stories, not as an escape from reality, but a restatement of reality's most fundamental truths.

At their heart, love stories are about not agreeing, the costs we pay when we don't agree, and the humanity we discover within ourselves when we have the courage to pay that price.

'In reading the Gospels,' Oscar Wilde wrote shaven-headed in Reading Gaol, '. . . I see the continual assertion of the imagination as the basis of all spiritual and material life, I see also that to Christ imagination was simply a form of love.'

Despite its invocation of Christ this is not a Christian idea, but one that flows forth through the troubadours and their courts of love, through Dante's *dolce stil novo* to Don Quixote's wild adventures being founded in love. Rilke, the tagger for Mitteleuropa, said something similar. Nothing touches a work of art so little as words of criticism, he wrote. Art is conceived in love and can only be apprehended through love.

A group of Manus Island contractors sent a statement to *Guardian Australia* describing Reza Barati as a 'gentle giant'. 'We read him children's books such as fairy tales and Reza always waited and looked forward to meeting with us and reading with him. He studied a lot,' they said.

'He used to always pick up bugs and moths off the ground and put them back in the garden, worried that someone would step on them. (The guys used to feed the moths to cane toad frogs around the compound for fun . . . There wasn't much else to do . . .) He used to try and stop them.'

They continued, 'Reza also always helped staff hand out medical slips and appointment slips to those in the same compound as him. He wanted to keep busy to avoid boredom and keep his mind active.'

There are no more fairy stories. The cane toads grow fatter. And Reza Barati's corpse lies in a Port Moresby morgue with a large hole in the back of its head as inexplicable, as shameful, as what our country has done.

For in the end all human life aspires to hope, the highest expression of which is love. Without hope, there is no future.

And love stories give me the courage to say in conclusion one thing: I do not agree. I do not.

'I could hear my heart beating,' wrote Ray Carver. 'I could hear everyone's heart. I could hear the human noise we sat there making, not one of us moving, not even when the room went dark.'

My Top Ten Tasmanian Novels

INAUGURAL BOISBOUVIER LECTURE,
MELBOURNE WRITERS FESTIVAL,
1 SEPTEMBER 2016

Every day we hear grim and grimmer news that suggests we are passing through the winter of the world. Everywhere man is tormented, the globe reels from multitudes of suffering and horror, and, worst, we no longer know with confidence what our answer might be. And yet we understand that the time approaches when an answer must be made or a terrible reckoning will be ours.

Perhaps this is what *BuzzFeed* meant when it featured an article with the title 'Ten Shitty Alternatives to Drinking Yourself to Death'. And in our age of clickbait— where our supposedly best newspapers feature articles like 'Six Hot Miniskirts Not to Wear to Your Father's

Funeral', '22 Photos to Restore Your Faith in Humanity Without You Actually Having to Do Anything About It', 'Top Five Crimes Favoured by Bilbies That Look Like Bilbies', or the almost as endearing 'Ten Ozzie Heroes Who Should Get a Fucking Medal'.

The last, I must admit, gives rise to a nagging question. Are the featured ten to be gonged for heroism or for copulation? There are enough holes in this for a One Nation senator to sense a NASA conspiracy.

In any case, in such an age my first thought was that I should get with the program, using vapid clichés like get with the program, and share with you my top ten Tasmanian novels.

Why?

Because these books were the ones in which I first discovered my world and myself. In them I discovered why writing matters.

Why, you may wonder, Tasmanian novels and not Australian?

And the seemingly sacrilegious answer is that I don't believe in national literature per se. I do believe in Australian writing, conceived mostly in obscurity, frequently in poverty, and almost always in adversity. I believe in that writing as important, as central, and as necessary.

But that's a different matter from a national litera-ture. Nations and nationalisms may use literature, but writing itself has nothing to do with national anythings. National traditions, national organisations, national prizes—all these and more are irrelevant. National any-things imply responsibilities, morals, ethics, politics.

And writing, at its best, exists beyond morality and politics. It is at its most enduring when, like a bird, or a beach, or a criminal bilby, it is completely irresponsible, committing the top five crimes favoured by writers that look like writing.

Meat may be murder but so too for a thousand years were books—one sheep or goat for every eight pages of vellum made from their skin. Gutenberg's revolution wasn't simply one of swapping a scribe's calligraphy for machine-pressed type. It was also swapping this highly expensive vellum for cheaper paper made out of rags, and, within half a century—most importantly, most revolutionary of all—it was swapping the Latin of the rulers for the vernacular of the ruled.

That had many consequences, not least the impetus it gave to the Reformation, the growth of science, the Enlightenment and democracy. It also fed powerfully into a new idea of a people bound by a language which evolved into the profoundly modern idea of a nation-state, bound together not by religion and monarch but by the common speech.

And the signet ring that common speech needed was literature. With the rise of the nation-state we witness as its necessary corollary those new figures—the national poet and, later, the national novelist, and the national literature they purportedly embody. A language is not, as is often claimed, a dialect with a navy. A nation, though, is a dialect with a literature.

And yet, that same literature is not a nation. It is not reducible to kitsch ideas like national spirit, nor is it bound by borders. A writer belongs both to the homeland of the people they love *and* to the universe of books, and can never renounce either.

This leads to the great paradox of national letters: writers who seem rooted in the particular but whose works are deemed universal. Arguably the greatest German writer of the twentieth century was Franz Kafka who was, of course, Czech. His tales of alienation, of guilt, of not being what you seem, could perhaps only have been written by a German-speaking Jew who grew up in a Catholic Slavic city such as Prague. But what that makes Kafka—German? Jewish? Czech? Slavic?—is perhaps not the point. He is a writer being true to the multitudes within himself that are one and many.

'Germany? But where is it?' asked Goethe and Schiller in a book of poems they co-authored in 1796. 'I don't know how to find such a country.'

Who of us does?

Goethe, the writer who, it has been said, invents not just German literature but Germany, finally realised his dream of Germany—and, with it, his inspiration to break with the stifling dead hand of French literature on German writing—in the work of an English playwright, William Shakespeare.

I say English, because until the ascension of James I to the throne in 1603, Shakespeare himself wrote for only one of the four countries that then comprised the British Isles, England, and was deeply concerned with Englishness. But after 1603, and the consequent union of the crowns of Scotland and England to form the nation of Britain, Shakespeare consciously became a British writer.

In Shakespeare's Elizabethan plays the word *England* appears 224 times, while the word *Britain* is used only twice. After 1603, the word *England* only appears twenty-one times in his Jacobean plays while the word *Britain* now appears twenty-nine times. The word *English*, used 132 times under Elizabeth I, is only used eighteen times under James. The word *British* was never used by Shakespeare at all until James came to the throne.

Shakespeare, like language itself, could be both things, neither thing and anything. His writings, in turn, were heavily influenced by Italian writers such as Petrarch and Boccaccio, and the French essayist Montaigne. In some ways their poetry and essays were more a fixed lodestone for him than the territory claimed by his monarch, a movable feast that prior to his birth had included much of France, and by his death incorporated through the crown the distant country of Scotland.

The history of letters is then a history of transnational ideas, styles and revolutions, which when they achieve fashion become celebrated and misrepresented as the reactionary virtues and stagnant spirit of nations.

It is ironic, then, that at the moment Australian writing began to announce itself as a force in the world, that at the moment it became perhaps our dominant indigenous cultural form, there ceased to be very much about it that might fit the thin idea of a national literature.

And that, to my mind, is no bad thing.

The corrupting notion of the great American novel is just one example of the end result of such empty thinking—books so huge that, like large plastic bags, they ought to be issued with warnings of death by asphyxiation if you take them to bed to read.

For over a century Australia wanted a national culture like those that had come to define European nations in the nineteenth century. The result was a mostly dreary colonial monoculture writ small in the image of the Melbourne and Sydney middle class. Caught between an imperial publishing culture that saw Australia as a consumer of English books but not a producer of writing on the one hand; and, on the other, the earnest national-ist expectations that there be some distinctly singular Australian voice, led to a mostly moribund culture of dreary confusions—Jindyworobaks on the one hand, a cringe towards Anglo modernists on the other.

And then, from the late 1960s, at the very moment globalism takes off, so too does Australian writing. This paradox, which you may have thought would lead to the death of any Australian writing, instead finally liberated it from the old nationalist arguments. Though the dead hand of the old intelligentsia lingered on in academia and literary journals, it was finished. Australian writing began to flourish, and at its best it wasn't a recognisably national literature in the European mould.

There isn't and there doesn't have to be a single united national project linking Benjamin Law to Tim Winton, that seeks resonances between Helen Garner and Omar Musa, that demands continuities between John Coetzee and Alexis Wright.

What matters is that we have these writers and their works in all their diversity, and so much more besides. And if we are freed of having to make a case for national worth or national failure in our books, so much the better. After all, writers are not the Australian swimming team, and we don't need missives from John Bertrand to make us feel better in the eyes of the nation.

Were though we to take the measure of whether Australian writing matters by what our political leaders think, we may feel a little like a Rio garage owner after Ryan Lochte visited. One simple piece of maths illustrates this point.

In 2014–15 our government spent $1.2 billion to keep innocent people in a state of torment and suffering so extreme it has been compared to torture. This destruction of human beings is deemed a major priority by our country, and is supported by both major parties. In the same year the same government spent a little less than $2.4 million on direct subsidy to Australian writers, the sum of whose work, it may be argued, whatever its defects and shortcomings, adds up to a collective good.

These figures are worth pondering. What Australia is willing to spend in one year to create a state-sponsored hell on earth for the innocent is what Australia would spend in 500 years supporting its writers. It may be worth considering as a cure for the chronic poverty of Australian writers that, in order to be 500 times more valuable to the nation than they presently are, they practise—instead of word processing—offshore processing, by aiding, abetting, participating in and covering up rape, murder, sexual abuse, beatings, child prostitution and suicide. Writers then would have a wholly admirable case to put to government for state sponsorship and political protection.

Who knows? Our prime minister might even turn up at a writers festival in a hi-vis jacket, a foie gras smear in jaffa icing. Would he be so moved by what he hears and sees as to put a few coins in our begging bowl?

But I am not in a begging mood. A writer may be fated to failure, poverty, slander, incomprehension and critical columns by Andrew Bolt. But a writer lives standing up, and they die kneeling. I am not arguing a case for more state support of writing. Heaven forbid that writers—who create wealth for others, jobs, and the only good news Australia seems to get these days internationally—should have any claim on the public purse, unlike, say, a failing, unprofitable and rigged entertainment like the Olympics.

But it is worth us pondering—if only for a moment— the question as to why our political class has such hostility towards writing. It may be that there is, buried in here, an inverse compliment: that Australian writing matters enough to power for power to want Australian writing to vanish for serving an economic purpose that doesn't accord with an economic ideology.

Bill Henson recently said the cultural cringe was back in Australia. I fear the situation may be worse than that. After all, the term cultural cringe denotes respect, if not for our own culture then at least for culture from other countries. But what if the end consequence of neoliberalism is a contempt for anything that can't be measured by money and status? What if there is no interest in any culture, no matter what country it comes from? When art and words exist solely as power's ornament, complement and cover?

For in our post-fact, post-truth, post-reason world, words seem to correspond ever less with the world as we experience it—as if the world itself is not what we experience but what power tells us we must accept as reality.

As Karl Rove put it about the Bush imperium in 2002, laying out the case for a new way of perceiving the universe, 'when we act, we create our own reality. And while you're studying that reality—judiciously, as you will—we'll act again, creating other new realities, which you can study too, and that's how things will sort out.'

In this view, reality is expressly the realm of power, and the rest of us become asylum seekers camped on its borders, reduced to wordless observers. Rove's prescient words could have been an instruction manual for Donald Trump, for Boris Johnson, for Pauline Hanson, for every Twitter troll and transnational marketing executive.

And in the face of this coming wave, it matters more than ever that we have ways of reconciling the experience of our lives with that of the larger world—a world in which we find false words are routinely used by power to deceive, dissemble and disempower. It matters that there might be a society where some are allowed the possibility of questioning, of not agreeing, of saying no, of proposing other worlds, of showing other lives.

It matters that there be voices in society speaking of what exists outside ideologies, that acknowledge both the beauty and the pain of this life, that celebrate the full complexity of what it is to be human without judgement, that aspire, finally, to give our lives meaning.

It is not that literature should prosecute a case or carry a message. It is that at its best it does neither. At its best it escapes the conventional categories of ideology, convention, taste and power; it subverts and questions and dares to rebel.

And though I didn't know it at the time, all of this was implicit in the first Tasmanian novel I ever read, and the first of my top ten Tasmanian novels. I discovered it at the age of twelve in a book spinner at my high school.

The high school had been built for a large housing commission suburb. It was violent, and the violence was unpredictable. One boy put a pair of scissors through another's hand. Another boy rammed a chisel up another's anus. A boy and his mate would use an air rifle to take pot shots at kids walking home from school. Gang beatings were commonplace. It had a name as the worst school in Tasmania. I am not sure if it was, but it wasn't a pleasant place.

On my third day at the school, in first year, I was sitting with two newly made friends on a bench seat hung off a brick wall, and we were eating our lunch. Some older boys walked by, including their gang leader, a stocky, powerful youth already sprouting sideburns. He halted, turned to us, and asked one of my new friends what he'd just said.

My friend had said nothing and said so. The stocky boy came over, leaned in, and with a movement I now understand must have been learned, gently cupped the boy's chin with his palm, almost a caress, before slamming the boy's head back, as hard as he could, into the brick wall three times. As the stocky boy turned and went to walk away, my other friend cried out, 'Why?' The stocky boy turned, smiled and said, 'Because I can.'

My world was never quite the same. It was far from the worst violence I would witness, but being the first it left its mark. Violence, I saw, didn't need a reason. And nor, in that school where bullying and violence were endemic, was it accountable. The teachers sought to maintain a rough order, not mete out justice. And over my four years at that school I came to see that, much as I hated it, this violence was also both a protest and an assertion of something deeply human; that the violence, sickening, despicable and damaging as it was, was also a strange assertion of freedom by people who had very little free agency.

I am not sure why I picked that book out that day. I remember it was very thin, and that this made it seem an attractive prospect. I was already an avid reader, but all that I read avidly were comics seasoned with some science fiction and a box of old penny Westerns. In contrast, the novel I had picked out was very strange to read. It was the first adult novel I ever read, and it had an indelible impact. If I didn't understand much of what it was about, that was also the way of much of the adult world that stood before me in all its enchantment. Rather than its impenetrable mystery making the book less compelling for me, it made it more so.

Reading *Wuthering Heights*, Dante Gabriel Rossetti observed, 'The action takes place in Hell, but the places, I don't know why, have English names.'

My experience with Albert Camus' *The Outsider* was not dissimilar: the characters have French names and the places an Algerian geography, but the action and spirit were, it was clear to me, entirely Tasmanian.

If I didn't understand much of Camus' *The Outsider*, Meursault's killing someone because of the heat made perfect sense to me because it made sense of the world I lived in. I understood the lack of judgement at the book's heart. I sensed the emotional damage that existed beyond what for a twelve-year-old was the novel's incomprehensible philosophy, because many of my friends at that school were odd and missing in ways that felt akin to Meursault. And I understood—only too well—the danger of telling the truth, which leads to the execution of Meursault. For I had learned the imperative of lies.

I understood a man who lives through his senses in a sensual world, who lives for the beach and the sea, and is undone by the heat of the sun, because my world—a child's world—had been a similar world; of beaches, of light, of heat, and also, in my case, of rain-forested wild lands and rivers.

Above all, I intimated one thing that excited me like nothing else: strange and alien as only a book like that could be to a twelve-year-old, it also felt true to something fundamental. To life. And to my life. And that was a truth I had never before experienced in books.

None of these ideas, it is fair to say, were to the fore in my copies of *The Phantom* or *Sun Sinking, Sioux Rising*. Later I would discover much more about Camus that made him even more the quintessential Tasmanian writer I had sensed him to be from the beginning. Camus was not a Parisian intellectual. Coming from Algeria he was himself the outsider, a man from what was viewed as a colony, who nevertheless did not view his world and his origins as less. He celebrated the beach, the sun, the world of the body and its pleasures.

Camus entered the European tradition of the novel at the moment when a nineteenth-century idea was at its most powerful—the idea of history as destiny. But it was an idea in which he saw implicit the dangers of totalitarianism. He opposed it with a radically different idea: that of the natural world as transcendent. 'In the depths of winter,' he wrote, 'I finally learned that there was, within me, an invincible summer.'

In Camus' writings I found my experience of Tasmania's rivers and forests, its great coasts and beaches, made sense of. They were what I had felt them to be: something inseparable; a world that lived in me and was indivisible from me unless I allowed it to be taken. Camus would later write that 'brought up surrounded by beauty which was my only wealth, I had begun in plenty'. And that beauty and plenty I had known in my life, and the name of it was freedom.

'The misery and greatness of this world: it offers no truths, but only objects for love,' Camus wrote in his journal. 'Absurdity is king, but love saves us from it.'

I was going to continue to list my other top Tasmanian novels, to show how I discovered other aspects of my Tasmania in each one, and how through their words I saw why writing matters. I was going to say how their worlds were already mine, and everything I read was everything I had already lived; that I passed through the writing of their books to the other side where there was some understanding and some reconciliation that was also a form of love for what my world was and for what all our worlds are. How it was as if, reading those books, I passed through the mystery to the truth, only to discover behind the truth an ever greater mystery.

I was going to tell you about so many Tasmanian writers—Cortázar, Márquez, Baldwin, Carver, Lispector, Rosa, Bolaño and Chekhov. I wrote pages on the wonderful palavering voice of Bohumil Hrabal's great novels; on the incomparable Faulkner and the shock of visiting his hometown in Mississippi, which until I smelled the dust and felt the heat and saw the kudzu I had not realised was also American. I was going to talk of Borges and his joyous pride in books being reality and a dream, and how that dream is the only reality worth living for, and how those games with time and chance were the same games played in the stories I grew up with. I was going to talk of Kafka and Conrad and Tolstoy and Hašek. I was going to talk, I came to realise, for several days and still not be done for it was, in the end, not a talk I was writing but a memoir in books.

And then I stumbled upon an extraordinary trove of anonymous Australian short stories. It was the most moving Australian writing I had read for some long time.

All around us we see words debased, misused and become the vehicles for grand lies. Words are mostly used to keep us asleep, not to wake us. Sometimes, though, writing can panic us in the same way we are sometimes panicked at the moment of waking: here is the day and here is the world and we can sleep no longer, we must rise and live within it.

This writing has woken me from a slumber too long. It has panicked me. The stories are very short, what might be called in another context flash fiction. Except they are true stories.

I suspect they will continue to be read in coming decades and even centuries, when my works and those of my colleagues are long forgotten. And when people read these stories, so admirable in their brevity, so controlled in their emotion, so artful in their artlessness—their use, for example, of the term NAME REDACTED instead of a character's actual name to better show that what is happening to a stranger is not an individual act but a universal crime—then, I suspect, their minds will be filled with so many questions about what sort of people Australians of our time were.

Let me read a handful to you. If you want to read them yourself, go to the *Guardian* website where these are published, along with 2000 others.

28 April 2015
At about 2129 hrs . . . [NAME REDACTED] approached staff in RPC3 area [NUMBER REDACTED]. She began to vomit. A strong smell of bleach was detected. A code blue was called.

IHMS medical staff attended and [NAME REDACTED] was transported by ambulance to RPC1 for further treatment . . . At 2220 hrs IHMS informed Control that as a result of their assessment it appears that [NAME REDACTED] has ingested Milton baby bottle sterilizing tablets.

28 September 2014

I was asked on Friday (26-9-2014) by a fellow teacher [NAME REDACTED] if I would sit with an asylum seeker [NAME REDACTED] who was sobbing. She is a classroom helper for the children . . . She reported that she has been asking for a 4 minute shower as opposed to 2 minutes. Her request has been accepted on condition of sexual favours. It is a male security person. She did not state if this has or hasn't occurred. The security officer wants to view a boy or girl having a shower.

12 June 2015

I [NAME REDACTED] met with [NAME REDACTED] in [REDACTED] at RPC1 . . . During the course of discussion [NAME REDACTED] disclosed that she had sex while in the community and that it had not been consensual.

CW asked [NAME REDACTED] if she had told anyone about this, [NAME REDACTED] stated that she had not told anyone other than CW that it was not consensual including IHMS. She stated that she did not tell IHMS that it was 'rape' as she did not want 'lots of questions' and if she said it was rape there would be 'lots of questions'. [NAME REDACTED] stated that she told the man 'no, no, no' and that the only man she wanted to have sexual relations with was her husband . . . the incident occurred during Open Centre and the man was Nauruan.

3 September 2015
[NAME REDACTED] was crying and was observed to be very shaken . . . [NAME REDACTED] reported that a Wilsons Security guard had just hit him. [NAME REDACTED] explained to [NAME REDACTED] that he was in tent [REDACTED] with [NAME REDACTED], [NAME REDACTED] and [NAME REDACTED] when a security guard entered and yelled at them, 'Why are you in here?'. [NAME REDACTED] then reported that the security guard grabbed him around the throat and hit his head against the ground twice. [NAME REDACTED] also said that the security guard threw a chair on him . . . [NAME REDACTED] asked [NAME REDACTED] to show her who the security guard was. The children lead CW to area 10 and pointed at a male security guard . . . [NAME REDACTED]

said 'he hit me'. [NAME REDACTED] then asked [NAME REDACTED] 'why did you hit me?'. [NAME REDACTED] then moved towards [NAME REDACTED] and in a raised voice responded 'did you come in here, you are not allowed in here, get out of here'. [NAME REDACTED] then lead [sic] the children out of area 10.

2 December 2014

At approximately 1125 hrs I was performing my duties as Whiskey 3.3 on a high watch in Tent [REDACTED] was alerted by an Asylum Seeker that female Asylum Seeker [NAME REDACTED] was trying to hang herself in Tent [NAME REDACTED]. I immediately responded. On arrival I saw [NAME REDACTED] holding [NAME REDACTED] up. [NAME REDACTED] appeared to have a noose around her neck. I called for a Code Blue straight away. I then assisted [NAME REDACTED] by untying the rope while [NAME REDACTED] held her and we took [NAME REDACTED] and placed her in the recovery position.

29 May 2015

[NUMBER REDACTED] y/o male was on a whiskey high watch from a previous incident . . . [NAME REDACTED] grabbed an insect replant

[sic] bottle and started drinking a small amount of its contents. CSO grabbed [NAME REDACTED] by the shoulders while his PSS offsider removed the bottle from [NAME REDACTED]'s hands. [NAME REDACTED] sat down and began sobbing over the incident.

15 January 2015
I (SCA CSPW [REDACTED 1]) was speaking with [REDACTED 2] in the grass above the security entrance of Area 9. [REDACTED 2] informed me that her husband [REDACTED 3] had reported 4 months ago to her that he had been in a car with his [NUMBER REDACTED] year old son with two [REDACTED] Wilson's Security officers. [REDACTED 2] stated that according to [REDACTED 3], [REDACTED 4] was sitting in-between himself and the security officer. [REDACTED 2] stated that this car was taking the two from Area 9 to IHMS RPC3. [REDACTED 2] alleged that [REDACTED 3] informed her that their son [REDACTED 4] had said to [REDACTED 3] that one Nauruan officer had put his hand up [REDACTED 4's] shorts and was 'playing with his bottom'. [REDACTED 3] . . . removed [REDACTED 4] from the middle of the car and placed [REDACTED 4] on his lap but did

not say anything as he feared the two [REDACTED] officers in the car with him . . . [REDACTED 2] informed me that approximately five months ago a [REDACTED 5] Officer had ran his hand down the back of her head and her head scarf and said to her 'if there is anything you want on the outside let me know. I can get you anything.'

26 June 2014
[REDACTED 1] informed SCA caseworker that his partner [REDACTED 2] tried to commit suicide by overdosing on medication pills. [REDACTED 1] stated that the couple changed rooms without permission. There were some family pictures on [the] wall of the old room and [REDACTED 2] was trying to rip them off the plastic wall . . . Wilson security officer entered the room and tried to stop [REDACTED 2] from damaging property. [REDACTED 1] stated that Wilson officer then stepped on her son's picture and kicked them and told them to shut up. After that [REDACTED 2] got upset and went to her room and took the pills.

5 May 2015
On morning bus run [NAME REDACTED] showed me a heart he had sewn into his hand using a needle and thread. I asked why and he said 'I don't

know' . . . [NAME REDACTED] is [NUMBER REDACTED] yrs of age.

27 September 2014

Witnesses informed CM that a young person had sewn her lips together, one of the officers [REDACTED 1] had gone to the young person's room to see her. The officer then went to his station with other officers and they all began laughing. Witnesses approached the officer asking what they were laughing about, the officers informed witnesses that they had told a joke and were laughing about it. Witnesses then stated that the young person's father had approached officers the next evening seeking an apology from officer [REDACTED 1] for laughing at his daughter. The young person's father at this time was informed that the officer [REDACTED 1] was at the airport, allegedly this is the reason the father then went and significantly self-harmed.

There is a connection between me standing here before you and a child sewing her lips together—an act of horror to make public on her body the truth of her condition. Because her act and the act of writing share the same human aspiration.

Everything has been done to dehumanise asylum seekers. Their names and their stories are kept from us.

They live in a zoo of cruelty. Their lives are stripped of meaning. And they confront this tyranny—our Australian tyranny—with the only thing not taken from them, their bodies. In their meaningless world, in acts seemingly futile and doomed, they assert the fact that their lives still have meaning.

And is this not the very same aspiration as writing?

In the past year, what Australian writer has written as eloquently of what Australia has become as asylum seekers have with petrol and flame, with needle and thread? What Australian writer has so clearly exposed the truth of who we are? And what Australian writer has expressed more powerfully the desire for freedom—that freedom which is also Australia?

That is why Australian writing is the smell of charring flesh as twenty-three-year-old Omid Masoumali burns his body in protest. The screams of twenty-one-year-old Hodan Yasin as she too sets herself alight. Australian writing is the ignored begging of a woman being raped. Australian writing is a girl who sews her lips together. Australian writing is a child who sews a heart into their hand and doesn't know why.

We are compelled to listen, to read. But more: to see.

The ancient Mesopotamians thought the footprints left by birds in the delta mud were the words of the gods. If the key to those words could be found, the gods could be seen. We need to use words to once more see each other for what we are: fellow human beings, no more, no less. To find the divine in each other, which is another way of saying that all we share is greater than our individual souls.

I say see, but of course there are no images. There are only leaked reports, which contradict so much of what the government claims. If there was an image of a woman just raped, of the back of murdered Reza Barati's bloody head; if there was just one image—*just* one—we would face a national crisis of honour, of meaning, of identity.

And though I wish I could, I cannot speak for Omid Masoumali. I cannot speak for Hodan Yasin. I cannot speak for the unnamed who have tried to kill themselves swallowing razor blades, hanging themselves with sheets, swallowing insecticides, cleaning agents and pills, and then were punished for doing so. I cannot speak for that girl with sewn lips. I can only speak for myself.

And I will say this: Australia has lost its way.

All I can think is this is not my Australia.

But it is.

It is too easy to ascribe the horror of what I have just read to a politician, to a party, or even to our toxic politics. These things, though, have happened because of a more general cowardice and inertia, because of conformity, because it is easier to be blind than to see, to be deaf than to hear, to say things don't matter when they do. Whether we wish it or not, these things belong to us, are us, and we are diminished because of them.

We have to accept that no Australian is innocent, that these crimes are committed in Australia's name, which is our name, and Australia has to answer to them, and so we must answer for them to the world, to the future, to our own souls.

We meekly accept what are not only affronts but also threats to our freedom of speech, such as the draconian section 42 of the *Australian Border Force Act*, which allows for the jailing for two years of any doctors or social workers who bear public witness to children beaten or sexually abused, to acts of rape or cruelty. The new crime is not crime, but the reporting of state-sanctioned violence. And only fools or tyrants argue that national security resides in national silence.

A nation-sized spit hood is being pulled over us. We can hear the guards' laughter, the laughter of the powerful at the powerless. We can hear once again the answer made all those years ago in a schoolyard as to why one human could hurt another, the real explanation of why the Australian government does what it does.

Because it can.

'All I say,' Camus writes in his great novel *The Plague*, 'is that on this earth there are pestilences and there are victims—and as far as possible one must refuse to be on the side of the pestilence.'

Our country's vainglorious boasts, of having a world-leading economy, of punching above its weight, of having the most liveable cities and so on, are worth nothing unless we can bear this truth. We can be a good nation or a trivial, fearful prison. But we cannot be both.

There is such a thing as a people's honour. And when it is lost, the people are lost. That is Australia today. If only out of self-respect, we should never have allowed to happen what has.

Every day that the asylum seekers of Nauru and Manus Island live in the torment of punishment without end, guilty of no crime, we too become a little less free. In their liberation lies our hope; the hope of a people that can once more claim honour in the affairs of this world.

For Camus, resistance was the heroism of goodness and kindness. 'It may seem a ridiculous idea,' he writes, 'but the only way to fight the plague is with decency.'

Camus understood moments such as those Australia is now passing through with asylum seekers not as wars that might be won, but aspects of human nature that we forget or ignore at our peril.

'The plague bacillus,' Camus writes, 'never dies or vanishes entirely . . . it waits patiently in bedrooms, cellars, trunks, handkerchiefs and old papers, and . . . the day will come when, for the instruction or misfortune of mankind, the plague will rouse its rats and send them to die in some well-contented city.'

We in Australia were well-contented. But now the rats are among us, the plague is upon us, and each of us must choose whether we are with the plague or against it.

A solidarity of the silenced, a resistance of the shaken, starts with what Camus understood was the necessity of weighing our words, by calling things by their proper names, and knowing that not doing so leads to the death and suffering of many.

It is by naming cruelty as cruelty, evil as evil, the plague as the plague.

The role of the writer in one sense is the very real struggle to keep words alive, to restore to them their proper meaning and necessary dignity as the means by which we divine truth. In this battle the writer is doomed to fail, but the battle is no less important. The war is only lost when language ceases to serve its most fundamental purpose, and that only happens when we are persuaded that writing no longer matters.

In all these questions I don't say that writing and writers are an answer or a panacea. That would be a nonsense. But even when we are silenced we must continue to write. To assert freedom. To find meaning.

With ink, with keyboard. With thread, with flame, with our very bodies.

Because writing matters. More than ever, it matters.

An Invitation
to Dream

NATIONAL PRESS CLUB SPEECH,
18 APRIL 2018

I told a friend the other day that I was to be speaking here in Canberra today and she told me a joke. A man is doubled over at the front of Parliament House throwing up. A stranger comes up and puts an arm around the vomiting man. 'I know how you feel,' the stranger says.

It's not a bad joke. But it felt familiar. I went searching my bookshelves, and finally found a variation of it in Milan Kundera's *The Book of Laughter and Forgetting*, set in communist Czechoslovakia in the dark years after the Prague Spring. In Kundera's version the two men are standing in Wenceslas Square.

Both jokes are about failing regimes that have lost the essential moral legitimacy governments need to govern. We don't have to like or agree with a government but we still accept it has the right to make decisions in our name. Until, that is, we don't. And it occurred to me that in both jokes it's not just those in immediate power but a whole system that is beginning to lose its moral legitimacy.

As a young man I was studying in England, which I didn't much enjoy, and spent most of my time in Yugoslavia, which I got to know through my wife's family who were Slovene, and which I enjoyed very much. Yugoslavia was then a communist dictatorship, but it occupied a curious place, halfway between the Soviet and capitalist system.

Yugoslavs were a well-educated, cultured people. But the system, like that of the Czechs, lost its legitimacy in the mid-1980s after Tito's death. A credit crisis became a full-blown economic, and then political, crisis. Opportunistic politicians, devoid of solutions to the nation's problems, instead pitched neighbour against neighbour. And suddenly nothing held.

I witnessed a country slide into inexplicable nationalisms and ethnic hatreds and, in a short space of time, into genocidal madness.

It made me realise at a young age that the veneer of civilised societies is very thin; a fragile thing that once broken brings forth monsters.

Czechoslovakia took a different route. After the final toppling of the system with the Velvet Revolution in

1989, the revolution's leader, Václav Havel, wrote presciently of how the West should not gloat over the fall of the old Soviet states. Eastern Europe was, he observed, simply a twisted mirror reflecting back a slightly more distorted image of what might come to prevail in the West. If the West did not learn from what that image portended of its future, it too might find itself one day facing a similar existential crisis.

In the heady 1990s Havel's warnings sounded absurd and overwrought. And yet it came to pass as Havel warned: the West did gloat, declaring the end of history and, in its triumphalism, dangerous new forces were allowed to fester unchecked, their scale and threat only becoming fully apparent in the past few years.

Now in Russia, in Turkey, in Poland, in Hungary and in the Czech Republic, we see the rise of the strongman leader, some, like Putin, already effectively dictators; others, like Erdoğan and Orbán, well on the way. In Slovakia a leading journalist was recently murdered after exposing links between leading Slovakian politicians and the Italian Mafia.

There are no saviours of democracy on the horizon. Rather, around the world we see a new authoritarianism that is always anti-democratic in practice, populist in appeal, nationalist in sentiment, fascist in sympathy and criminal in disposition. It tends to spew a poisonous rhetoric aimed against refugees, Muslims and increasingly Jews, and it is hostile to truth and those who speak it, most particularly journalists to the point, more and more frequently, of murder.

And yet this new authoritarianism is resonant with so many, acting as it does as a justification for rule by a few wealthy oligarchs and corporations, and as an explanation for the growing immiseration of the many.

In Australia though we feel ourselves, as ever, a long way away. We feel we are somehow immune from these dangerous currents. After all, we have had routine forays into populist extremism from the mid-1990s, with the likes of Hansonism, without it ever threatening our democracy. Our politics may be dreadful, a black comedy pregnant with collapse, its actors exhausted, without imagination or courage or principle, solely obsessed with pillaging the tawdry jewels of office and fleeing into distant sinecures as ambassadors or high commissioners, or with paid-up Chinese board posts, while outside the city burns. But it is all very far from a dictatorship.

Our society grows increasingly more unequal, more disenfranchised, angrier, more fearful. Even in my hometown of Hobart, as snow settles on the mountain there is the deeply shameful spectacle of a tent village of the homeless, the number of which increases daily. We sense the rightful discontent of the growing numbers locked out from a future. From hope.

Instead of public debate, scapegoats are offered up—the boatperson, the queue-jumper, the Muslim—a xenophobia both parties have been guilty of playing on for electoral benefit for two decades. Instead of new ideas and new visions we are made to wallow in threadbare absurdities and convenient fictions: Australia Day, the world's most liveable cities, secure borders.

Our institutions are frayed. Our polity is discredited, and almost daily discredits itself further. The many problems that confront us, from housing to infrastructure to climate change, are routinely evaded. Our screens are filled with a preening peloton of potential leaders, but nowhere is there to be found leadership.

Hölderlin, the great nineteenth-century poet, wrote of the 'mysterious yearning toward the chasm' that can overtake nations. Increasingly, one can sense that yearning in the overly heated rhetoric of some Australian politicians and commentators. That yearning can overtake Australia as easily as it has many other countries, damaging our democratic institutions, our freedoms and our values.

Politics, which ought to have as its highest calling the task of holding society together, of keeping us away from the chasm, has retreated to repeating divisive myths that have no foundation in the truth of what we are as a nation, and so finally only serve to contribute to the forces that could yet destroy us. Or worse yet, openly stoking needless fear and, with the refugee issue, a xenophobia for short-term electoral advantage.

The consequence is a time bomb which simply needs as a detonator what every other country has had and we have not: hard times. But hard times will return. And when they do what defence will we have should a populist movement that trades on the established scapegoats arises? An authoritarian party with a charismatic leader that uses the poison with which the old myths are increasingly pregnant to deliver itself power?

The challenge that faces us, the grave and terrifying challenge, is to transform ourselves as a people. This fundamental challenge is not policy, it is not franking credits, nor is it tax giveaways or rail links; necessary or not as these things may be. It is to realise that if we don't create for ourselves a liberating vision founded in the full truth of who we are as a people, we will find ourselves, in a moment of crisis, suddenly entrapped in a new authoritarianism wearing the motley of the old lies.

For we are a people of astonishing perversity.

We are an ancient country that insists on thinking itself new. We are a modern nation that insists our recent arrangements are so time-honoured that none of them can ever be changed. We are a complex country that insists on being simple-minded. We regard simplicity as a national virtue, and when coupled with language unimpeded by the necessity for thought, it is regarded as evidence of strong character. Which may explain our treasurer Scott Morrison, but little else.

And for the past two decades we have doubled down and doubled down again on old myths—lies—that become more dangerous the longer we allow them to go unchallenged.

Six days from now, on the eve of Anzac Day, the prime minister, Malcolm Turnbull, will launch a war memorial-cum-museum in France. Costing an extra-ordinary $100 million, the Monash Centre is reportedly the most expensive museum built in France for many years. It will honour those Australians who so tragically lost their lives on the Western Front in World War I and, more generally, the 62,000 Australians who died in World War I.

Would that someone might whisper into the prime minister's ear the last lines of Wilfred Owen's poem about those same fatal trenches:

> My friend, you would not tell with such high zest
> To children ardent for some desperate glory,
> The old Lie: *Dulce et decorum est*
> *Pro patria mori.*

Owen's last Latin phrase—the old lie, as he puts it—is from the Roman poet Horace: 'It is sweet and fitting to die for one's country.'

Except the Australians didn't even die for Australia. They died for Britain. For *their* empire. Not our country. A double lie then: a lie within a lie.

But, as Tony Abbott asked when, as prime minister, he announced the building of the museum, what was the alternative in Britain's time of need?

Well, we might answer, staying home for one thing, and not dying in other people's wars.

And yet the horrific suffering of so many Australians for distant empires has now become not a terrible warning, not a salient story of the blood sacrifice that must be paid by nations lacking independence, not the unhappy beginning of an unbroken habit but, bizarrely, the purported origin story of us as an independent people.

The growing state-funded cult of ANZAC will see $1.1 billion spent by the Australian government on war memorials between 2014 and 2028. Those who lost their lives deserve honour—I know from my father's experience how meaningful that can be. But when veterans struggle for recognition and support for war-related suffering, you begin to wonder what justifies this expense; this growing militarisation of national memory or, to be more precise, a forgetting of anything other than an official version of war as the official version of our country's history, establishing dying in other people's wars as our foundation story.

And so, the Monash Centre, for all its good intentions, for all the honour it does the dead, is at heart a centre for forgetting. It leads us to forget that the 62,000 young men who died in World War I died far from their country in service of one distant empire fighting other distant empires. It leads us to forget that not one of those deaths it commemorates was necessary. Not 62,000. Not even one.

Lest we forget we will all chant next week, as we have all chanted for a century now. And yet it is as if all that chanting only ensures we remember nothing. If we remembered would we, one hundred years later, still allow our young men to be sent off to kill or be killed in distant conflicts defending yet again not our country, but another distant empire, as we have in Iraq and Afghanistan?

If all that chanting simply reinforces such forgetting, then what hope have we now in negotiating some independent, safe path for our country between the growing tension of another dying empire, the American, and the rising new empire of the Chinese? Because instead of learning from the tragedies of our past, we are ensuring that we will learn nothing.

The forgetting extends to the horrific suffering of war. The prime minister who will, no doubt, speak sincerely and movingly of the torn bodies and broken lives of the Australians who fell in France, is also the same prime minister who wants to see the Australian arms industry become one of the world's top ten defence exporters, seeking to boost exports to several countries, including what was described as 'the rapidly growing markets in Asia and the Middle East', in particular the United Arab Emirates, a country accused of war crimes in Yemen.

Anzac Day, which is a very important day for my family, was always a day to remember all my father's mates who didn't make it home. But it was also a moment to ponder the horror of war more generally. But, of late, Anzac Day has become enshrouded in cant and entangled in dangerous myth. If this seems overstated, ponder the bigoted bile that attended Yassmin Abdel-Magied's tweet last Anzac Day in which she posted 'LEST. WE. FORGET. (Manus, Nauru, Syria, Palestine . . .)'

I read this as a plea for compassion drawing on the memory of a national trauma.

Most refugees on Manus Island and Nauru are fleeing war. Syria has half a million dead and more than eleven million people exiled internally and externally because of war, and Palestinians, whatever position one takes, suffer greatly from ongoing conflict.

And yet, as the attacks on Abdel-Magied showed, some were seeking to transform Anzac Day into a stalking horse for racism, misogyny and anti-Islamic sentiment. For hate, intolerance and bigotry. For all those very forces that create war. The great disrespect to Anzac Day wasn't the original tweet but the perverted attacks made on it in, of all things, the name of the dead. Those who think they honour Anzac Day by forgetting contemporary victims of war only serve to make a tragic mockery of all that it should be.

Freedom means Australia facing up to the truth of its past.

We should, of course, question these things more. We could ask why—if we were actually genuine about remembering patriots who have died for this country— we would not first spend $100 million on a museum honouring the at least 65,000 estimated Indigenous dead who so tragically lost their lives defending their country here in Australia in the frontier wars of the 1800s? Why is there nowhere in Australia telling the stories of the massacres, the dispossession and the courageous resistance of these patriots?

The figure of 65,000, I should add, is one arrived at by two academics at the University of Queensland, and applies only to Indigenous deaths in Queensland. If their methodology is correct, the numbers for the Indigenous fallen nationally must be extraordinarily large.

As one prominent commentator noted, 'Individually and collectively, it was sacrifice on a stupendous scale. We should be a nation of memory, not just of memorials, for these are our foundation stories. They should be as important to us as the ride of Paul Revere, or the last stand of King Harold at Hastings, or the incarceration of Nelson Mandela might be to others.'

The commentator was Tony Abbott, announcing the French museum and speaking of the dead of World War I.

And yet how can his argument be said not to also hold for the Indigenous dead? After all, Sir John Monash became a great military leader in spite of considerable prejudice. And so too Pemulwuy and Jandamarra.

Of course, such a reasonable and necessary proposal as a museum for the Indigenous fallen would at first be greeted with ridicule and contempt. Because in the deepest, most fundamental way we are not free of our colonial past. Freedom exists in the shadow of memory. For Australia to find out what freedom means it has to face up to the truth of its past. And it's time we decided to accept what we are and where we come from, because only in that truth can we finally be free as a people.

Sixty years ago, the scientific consensus was that Indigenous Australians had been in Australia for only 6000 years. But, through a series of breath-taking discoveries, science has confirmed what Indigenous people always knew: that they have been here far, far longer, stretching back, at last count, at least 60,000 years.

It makes you wonder if the $500 million earmarked for renovating the Australian War Memorial would not be more wisely spent on a world-class national Indigenous museum that honours a past unparalleled in human history. Surely, when we have the oldest continuous civilisation on Earth, such a major institution is central to our understanding of ourselves as a people? Is it not necessary, and fundamental to us as a nation?

It is, after all, extraordinary, and beyond a disgrace that there is in the twenty-first century no museum telling that extraordinary story, so that all Australians might know it, so that the world might share in it, and so that we might learn something of the struggle and achievement, the culture and unique civilisations that were and are Indigenous Australia.

We have turned our back on this profound truth again and again, because to acknowledge it is also to acknowledge the other great truth of Australia: that the prosperity of contemporary Australia was built on the destruction of countless Indigenous lives up to the present day and, with them, dreamings, songlines, languages, alternative ways of comprehending not only our extraordinary country but the very cosmos.

And yet, if we were to have the courage and largeness to acknowledge as a nation both truths about our past, we would discover a third truth; an extraordinary and liberating truth for our future, about who we are and where we might go.

We would discover that though this land and its

people were colonised, a 60,000-year-old civilisation is not so easily snuffed out. The new people who came to Australia, in their dealings with black Australia, were also indigenised and, in the mash up, Indigenous values of land, of country, of time, of family, of space and of story became strong among non-Indigenous Australians. Indigenous ways, forms and understandings permeated our mentality in everything from Australian Rules football to our sense of humour.

As much as there was a process of colonisation, there was also a history of indigenisation—a frequently repressed, often violent, process in which a white under-class took on many black ways of living and sometimes, more fundamentally, thinking and feeling, in which may be traced continuities that extend back into deep time.

We would discover that we are not Europeans, nor are we Asians. That we are not a new country. We are, in the first instance, a society that begins in deep time. That is the bedrock of our civilisation as Australians, our birthright, and if we would accept it, rather than spurn it, we might discover so many new possibilities for ourselves as a people.

My own island is a good example of both processes. There took place what was described, not by a contemporary left-wing academic but an 1830s Van Diemonian attorney-general, as 'a war of extermination' of the island's Aboriginal people. A terrible war of which fewer than one hundred people survived, the forebears of today's 25,000-strong Palawa population.

To this day Tasmanian society is shaped by the tragedy of a land where the English, as a ship's captain's wife, Rosalie Hare, confided in her diary in 1828, 'consider the massacre of these people an honour'.

But it was, for a critical time, also a land where many ex-convicts, to quote a contemporary witness, 'dress in kangaroo skins without linen and wear sandals made of seal skins. They smell like foxes.' They live in 'bark huts like the natives, not cultivating anything, but living entirely on kangaroos, emus, and small porcupines'. In coming to understand how to live in this strange new world, they took on Aboriginal partners, ways of life and thinking.

No less an authority than John West, the first official editor of the *Sydney Morning Herald*, wrote in 1856 that whites living outside of the two major Van Diemonian settlements 'had a way of life somewhat resembling that of the Aborigines'.

The bush became freedom, and for a time the Van Diemonian authorities feared a jacquerie in which the ex-convicts would make common cause with the Aboriginal population.

It was a messy, often brutal, inescapably human response to extraordinary times and places, out of which emerged a new people. It was a revolution of sense and sensibilities so extraordinary it is even now hard to fully compass its liberating dimensions.

If this history is frequently terrible, it is also, finally, a history of hope for us all. For it shows we are not dispossessed Europeans, but a muddy wash of peoples made anew in the meeting of a pre-industrial, pre-modern European culture with a remarkable Indigenous culture and an extraordinary natural world.

George Orwell once said that the hardest thing to see is what is in front of your face.

This is what is in front of ours.

We became our own people, not a poor imitation of elsewhere.

We pretend that our national identity is a fixed, frozen thing, but Australia is a molten idea. We have only begun to think of ourselves as Australians within living memory. There was no legal concept of an Australian citizen until 1948. Twenty years later, the Australian population was still divided into three official categories by the Australian Bureau of Statistics in its official year book—British: born in Australia; British: born overseas; and foreign.

Indigenous Australia wasn't even recorded as a general category.

Indigenous Australia has, after great thought and wide discussion, asked that its wishes be heard, and that these, first and foremost, take the form of an advisory body to parliament—a body that would be recognised in the Constitution.

'What a gift this is that we give you,' Galarrwuy Yunupingu has said, 'if you choose to accept us in a meaningful way.'

The gift we are being offered is vast; the patrimony of 60,000 years and with it the possibilities for the future that it opens up to us. We can choose to have our beginning and our centre in Indigenous culture. Or we can choose to walk away, into a misty world of lies and evasions, pregnant with the possibility of future catastrophe.

But this gift needs honouring in what Yunupingu calls a 'meaningful way'. It needs honouring with institutions, with monuments, with this profound history being made central in our account of ourselves and, above all, with what the Indigenous people have asked for repeatedly: constitutional recognition.

In truth, we can no longer go forward without addressing this matter. We cannot hope to be a republic if this is not at the republic's core, because otherwise we are only repeating the error of the colonialists and the federationists before us.

At a moment when democracy around the world is imperilled, we are being offered, with the Uluru Statement, the chance to complete our democracy, to make it stronger, more inclusive and more robust. And we would be foolish to turn that offer down.

That saying the things that I have said today might be deemed unreasonable, or shrill, or far-fetched, should remind us all of how intolerable the situation remains in this country for Indigenous people. How unbearable it must be for Indigenous people to know that their patrimony, their 60-millennia-old culture, which they are willing to share, which has shaped and continues to shape much of what is best in Australia, will, however, continue to be treated as marginal and they, again, be humiliated.

Even if you have no respect for Indigenous Australia, you should care for the future of your country. And now more than ever we need ways of bringing us together, not as, for example, Australia Day presently does— dividing us. We need a large and open vision sustained in truth, not myths that encourage dangerous illusions.

I know these are large ideas. But perhaps they are the ideas for these times. None of these things are easy. None will be quickly arrived at.

But the alternative is worse; the alternative is the slow collapse, it is the many cracks which are already appearing; the inequality; the grounds for an authoritarian revolt, for a hopelessly divided country. The alternative is Hölderlin's yearning for the chasm.

Definitions belong to the definer not the defined. For twenty years Australians lived with the definition that they were selfish, xenophobic, self-interested and incapable of being roused on larger issues.

But the marriage equality debate proved it was not so. Since the marriage equality vote, it's clear that Australians are not the mean and pinched people we had been persuaded and bluffed for so many years to believe that we were.

We are not small-minded bigots. We are, as it turns out, people who care. We are people who feel and who think. Australia is not a fixed entity, a collection of outdated bigotries and reactionary credos, but rather the invitation to dream, and this country—our country—belongs to its dreamers.

And if after more than twenty years of groundhog day we are finally ready to once more go forward as a people, it's time our dreamers were brought in from the cold and, with them, Galarrwuy Yunupingu's great gift of the Australian dreaming.

Endnotes

4 peptides
In 2013, Australian sport was consumed with a doping scandal that had engulfed AFL club Essendon, as evidence mounted of the club having run a program administering banned peptides to its players.

25 those whose job is to find truth . . .
The Australian, among many media outlets, reported on 29 January 2014 that Prime Minister Tony Abbott had attacked the ABC on radio station 2GB, accusing it of taking 'an anti-Australian stance in its reporting'. Referring to reports of alleged mistreatment of asylum seekers by RAN personnel, the prime minister declared 'you shouldn't be critical of your own country'.

> It dismays Australians when the national broadcaster appears to take everyone's side but our own and I think it is a problem . . . You would like the national broadcaster to have . . . at least some basic affection for the home team.

26 no longer wise for a public figure to express concern . . .
On 3 February 2014, the president of the Australian Human Rights Commission, Gillian Triggs, launched the National Inquiry into Children in Immigration Detention to 'investigate the ways in which life in immigration detention affects the health, well-being and development of children'. And with that began one of the most sustained and vicious attacks on a public official in Australian history. The highest levels of the government, duly echoed and amplified by far right commentators, made every effort politically, bureaucratically and publicly to discredit and destroy a public servant doing their duty.

26 Reza Barati

A twenty-three-year-old Iranian Kurd asylum seeker, who was murdered during a riot on Manus Island on 17 February 2014 when security guards and locals attacked the Manus refugee detention centre. News of his murder only became widespread in Australia on 22 February (the day before this speech was delivered). Two New Guinea men were later found guilty of Barati's murder. According to the judge, Nicholas Kirriwom, there were other people involved in the killing who had not been charged. These are understood to include two Australian employees of security contractors G4S. A subsequent Senate inquiry found the violence 'eminently foreseeable', spoke of human rights violations, and concluded that the Australian government had failed in its duty to protect asylum seekers, including Barati.

According to fellow Manus inmate and Barati's friend, Behrouz Boochani:

> immigration had fomented hate against the refugees among the locals. For days on end after the riot the Manusian residents and local guards told the refugees that they were just following orders. They claimed they were not to blame and it was all the machinations of the Australians . . . There was just one objective to their plans: to make the refugees return back to their countries by giving them a severe beating . . .
>
> The riot occurred over two consecutive nights . . . On the second night the power was cut and the prison became completely dark. Some local people together with G4S guards attacked the prison. It was there that over 100 refugees were severely injured, one person was shot, one person had their throat slit . . . and Reza was killed . . .
>
> Reza was a kind-hearted and compassionate human being . . . He was essentially nothing more than an ordinary youth with the kind of dreams that every single young man from every single culture has for his future. He died at the hands of people who he requested to provide him protection and in a prison on a remote island.

theguardian.com/commentisfree/2018/feb/17/four-years-after-reza-baratis-death-we-still-have-no-justice

27 'We accept that sometimes in difficult circumstances, difficult things happen'
Licensed from the Commonwealth of Australia under a Creative Commons Attribution 4.0 International Licence.
http://pmtranscripts.pmc.gov.au/release/transcript-23094

27 'kicked, beaten with batons and pipes, burned with hot wires and cigarettes, submerged in a barrel of water until she thought she would drown, suffocated by having a petrol-soaked plastic bag put over her head, before being repeatedly raped by men in [Sri Lankan] army uniform', the torture and rape going on for 20 days 'before a relative could find her and pay a bribe for her release'
Frances Harrison: https://www.bbc.com/news/world-asia-24849699

30 Manus Island contractors
theguardian.com/world/2014/feb/21/manus-dead-asylum-seeker-iranian-reza-berati

39 Ryan Lochte
An American swimmer competing at the 2016 Rio de Janeiro Olympics, Lochte achieved momentary global fame after his claim to have been robbed at gunpoint at a Rio petrol station late one night was exposed as a lie. It was revealed that Lochte, with some teammates, had rather vandalised and urinated on a petrol station, and then sought to buy off security guards.

40 Bill Henson
In a profile in the *Sydney Morning Herald* of 29 March 2016, the leading Australian artist was paraphrased as saying 'that the Cultural Cringe is back with a vengeance. He feels we live in a country with so little interest in the arts that governments will persist with destructive policies solely because of a lack of interest—or a lack of influence as an election issue.'

41 'when we act, we create our own reality. And while you're studying that reality—judiciously, as you will—we'll act again, creating other new realities, which you can study too, and that's how things will sort out'
Ron Suskind: https://www.nytimes.com/2004/10/17/magazine/faith-certainty-and-the-presidency-of-george-w-bush.html

69 Yassmin Abdel-Magied
On Anzac Day in 2017, Yassmin Abdel-Magied posted 'LEST. WE. FORGET. (Manus, Nauru, Syria, Palestine . . .)' on her Facebook page. National controversy ensued. Conservative politicians such as Barnaby Joyce, Eric Abetz, Peter Dutton, Mitch Fifield and Tony Abbott were outraged. George Christensen called for Abdel-Magied to consider self-deportation. The *Daily Telegraph* branded it 'a sickening insult to the nation's war dead'. Attacks on Abdel-Magied by right-wing columnists and via social media were vicious and sustained.

70 65,000 estimated Indigenous dead
theguardian.com/commentisfree/2014/jul/15/why-the-number-of-indigenous-deaths-in-the-frontier-wars-matters

70 'Individually and collectively, it was sacrifice on a stupendous scale. We should be a nation of memory, not just of memorials, for these are our foundation stories. They should be as important to us as the ride of Paul Revere, or the last stand of King Harold at Hastings, or the incarceration of Nelson Mandela might be to others'
Licensed from the Commonwealth of Australia under a Creative Commons Attribution 4.0 International Licence.
http://pmtranscripts.pmc.gov.au/release/transcript-23446

73 'a war of extermination'
Nicholas Clements, *The Black War*, (University of Queensland Press, 2014) p.142. The phrase was often used. 'Exterminationist sentiment was certainly common,' writes Clements (ibid.).

74 'massacre of these people an honour'
Clements, op. cit., pp.185-6.

74 'dress in kangaroo skins'
James Boyce, *Van Diemens Land*, (Black Inc, 2008) p.102. Boyce has much of great interest to say on these themes, particularly in pp.101–125.

74 'a way of life somewhat resembling that of the Aborigines'
Boyce, ibid., p.104.

Acknowledgements

With thanks to Perth Writers Festival, the Melbourne Writers Festival and the National Press Club for inviting me to deliver these speeches; Nick Feik at *The Monthly* and Lucy Clark at *The Guardian* for first publishing them with passion and belief; and Nikki Christer and Rosie Pearce at Penguin Random House for helping me breathe life into old embers and from them create this book.